COSMIC COMPANION

WORKBOOK

A Guide for Incorporating Astrology
Into Your Life

THE PULP GIRLS

ROCK
POINT

INTRODUCTION

Why, hello there, cosmic hottie! Welcome to a journey into, well, you! Whether you're an old pro at astrology or a fresh-faced newbie, you're holding in your hands not only a gorgeous guide to self-discovery, but also a fun, chill, interactive workbook! We've crafted this workbook to help you learn more about astrology and as a space you can use to retreat and reflect.

The cosmic forces at work all around us might be deep and magical and mysterious, but they're also straight-up fascinating. And yeah, if you've started looking into it, you've probably realized that astrology can be an incredibly complex subject, one that feels more and more complicated as you get deeper into it. Thankfully, you don't have to *get* it all instantly. You can learn about your placements at your own speed. Some stuff you'll resonate with right away, while other stuff won't make sense until you spend time exploring your own inner self. And best of all: there's no reason learning about astrology can't be fun!

So how does this work? First things first: get yourself something to write with, and maybe some colored pencils or markers . . . whatever fun decorating items you have at hand can help make this workbook truly your own! If you are new to astrology, we suggest going in order to better understand your birth chart, but there's really no wrong way to use this book, y'all. You can also flip open to a random page or choose an activity that calls to you in the moment. Or, you can repeat the same activities as you feel called to them. If you run out of room to write, feel free to use a separate piece of paper or a blank journal.

Each chapter is loosely structured to build upon the last one, with a self-check-in at the end of each one to help you keep track of your journey. You will also notice each check-in page includes a confidence meter for you to color in as you build up your astrological knowledge.

Journal Checklist

- [ ] This journal, ofc!
- [ ] Writing tools
- [ ] Coloring Utensils
- [ ] Your birth date, time, and place
- [ ] Your creativity!
- [ ] An amazing playlist to vibe to
- [ ] A burning desire for astrology

ASTROLOGY 101

There are a lot of moving parts in astrology. This journey into the world of the zodiac typically begins with the Sun sign, which makes sense, since this is the placement that horoscopes usually refer to, and it's the easiest one to figure out. All you need is a birth date and, voilà: Sun sign discovered, and the door to your astrology journey unlocked. Getting into astrology gives you a whole new way to talk about yourself, your friends, and your relationships. Realizing that the friend with the *best* advice is a Virgo? And that totally self-assured crush of yours is a Leo? Yeah, things will just start making sense suddenly. Once you know, you just know. You're equipping yourself with a totally new language for examining yourself and your relationships.

But hold on, there are only twelve recognized zodiac signs, and there are way more than twelve personality types out there. How does that work? Well, darlin', Sun signs are just the tip of the astrological iceberg! There's a lot more to a person than where the Sun was when they took their first breath. We've got the whole solar system at play in each and every person, not to mention the many astrological house systems or unique aspects. Isn't that kinda totally beautiful? Learning about each zodiac sign allows you to understand how all your placements come together to make you uniquely you.

This chapter will have your birth chart, as well as an overview of the signs, elements, and modalities. We'll delve into the planets and houses in the following chapter. Having a good feel for the signs is important, since we all have each one somewhere in our birth charts. The deeper you delve into your own chart, the more you'll notice each sign's influence on an area of your life. It's complex, but that doesn't mean it can't be fun! We're here for you, cutie.

YOUR BIRTH CHART

The best advice when getting into the wild world of astrology is to start simple. In this case, that's right at the beginning: your birth. Your birth chart, also referred to as a natal chart, is truly the key to unlocking all your astrological information. It is far and away the most important piece of your astrological journey. Think of your birth chart as a beautiful picture of what was going on in the heavens at the exact moment you took your first breath of life. (So yes, this includes natural births, C-sections, and whatever else.)

To calculate your birth chart, you will need your date of birth, time of birth, and place of birth. You can do this by simply typing out "birth chart calculator" on Google. We like to use Astrodienst—it offers a lot of chart types and allows you to save charts for future reference.

Note: Your birth certificate is the best source for your birth information. If you don't have access to your birth certificate, there are a few things you could try to get your exact time of birth. Of course, asking your mom may be the easiest. If that's not an option, and you know where you were born, you can order a long-form birth certificate and specifically request your birth time be included on it. If all else fails, look into birth time rectification, where an astrologer works backward through the events of your life to find your likely birth time.

Once you have your chart calculated, take a minute and sit with it. Look at this chart as a method of examining all areas of your life, including how you act, react, and interact. Use this chart as a tool for deciphering all the pieces of your personality. Honestly, there's truly nothing more powerful than knowing yourself, and your birth chart is the key to understanding your personality, your needs, your drives . . . everything that makes you, you!

Print out that birth chart and paste or tape it in here, or take a screenshot and save it to your favorites in Photos. If you want to get wild, you can get out the protractor and compass and draw out your own chart!

ALL THOSE SYMBOLS!

Before we dive into the signs, let's all take a quick second to celebrate you being so dang amazing . . . and to decipher all those symbols in your chart, also known as glyphs. Because you probably want to be able to tell what planet you have in what sign, right? As you learn the glyphs, practice drawing them into the third column to help you remember them and have some fun!

THE SIGNS

Glyph	Sign	Your Turn!		Glyph	Sign	Your Turn!
♈	Aries			♎	Libra	
♉	Taurus			♏	Scorpio	
♊	Gemini			♐	Sagittarius	
♋	Cancer			♑	Capricorn	
♌	Leo			♒	Aquarius	
♍	Virgo			♓	Pisces	

THE PLANETS & ASCENDANT

Glyph	Placement	Your Turn!
☉	Sun	
☽	Moon	
A^{SC}	Ascendant	
☿	Mercury	
♂	Mars	
♀	Venus	
♃	Jupiter	
♄	Saturn	
♅	Uranus	
♆	Neptune	
♇	Pluto	

THE SIGNS

You can't talk astrology without knowing the zodiac signs. Everyone has these signs and their energies somewhere in their birth chart. That's why it's important to know not just your Sun sign traits, but those of all twelve signs. Like everything else, the signs exist on a spectrum: there are strengths and weaknesses, light traits, and shadow traits for each.

Luckily, you don't have to memorize all this to get your astrology journey going. Feel free to flip back to this section whenever you need a reference for the signs. The more you work with astrology, the more you'll come to understand it, we promise!

Cosmic Tip

We've given the usual dates for each sign, but these can change by a day or so depending on the year. If your birthday falls on a cusp, or division, between the signs, you should definitely be checking your birth chart for an accurate Sun sign. Everyone has one Sun placement, which is influenced by the rest of their chart.

ARIES

March 21–April 19

Ruled by Mars, represented by the ram, Aries is big
on action, competition, and taking the initiative. This sign colors
a placement with a lot of passion and eagerness. When cardinal
fire sign Aries shows up in a chart, think enthusiasm,
impulsiveness, and perhaps even forcefulness.

Strengths	Weaknesses	Element	Modality
Energetic, Passionate, Sincere, Good-Natured	Aggressive, Competitive, Reckless, Careless	Fire	Cardinal

**Aries people are all about claiming their power!
When did you last jump into something wholeheartedly?**

TAURUS

April 20–May 20

Taurus is ruled by Venus and represented by the bull,
making Tauruses extremely resolute, chill, and sensual.
They love to indulge all five senses, enjoying all life has to offer.
When Taurus shows up in a placement, think reliability,
reassurance, and, sometimes, stubbornness.

Strengths	Weaknesses	Element	Modality
Trustworthy, Grounded, Determined, Realistic	Stubborn, Possessive, Anxious, Change-Averse	Earth	Fixed

Tauruses seek to taste, touch, smell, hear, and see everything.
Down to the detail, what is your perfect day?

....

....

....

....

....

....

....

....

GEMINI

May 21–June 20

Ruled by Mercury, Gemini's symbol is the twins. Geminis have a reputation for being very mercurial and a bit of a shapeshifter, subtly changing their personae depending on the audience. When Gemini shows up in a chart, think communication, curiosity, and maybe even recklessness.

Strengths	Weaknesses	Element	Modality
Funny, Versatile, Charismatic, Expressive	Changeable, Flighty, Contradictory, Easily Bored	Air	Mutable

Geminis flit from interest to interest with ease.
What are you passionate about right now?

CANCER

June 21–July 22

Represented by the crab and ruled by the Moon,
Cancers are known for being intuitive, nurturing, and
protective. That hard outer shell protects a soft, tender heart within.
With Cancer placements, think tenderness, hidden strengths,
and perhaps even volatile emotionality.

Strengths	Weaknesses	Element	Modality
Compassionate, Comforting, Empathetic, Nourishing	Indirect, Melancholy, Codependent, Reclusive	Water	Cardinal

Cancers intuitively tap into a deep well of creativity.
How does the Universe speak to you?

LEO

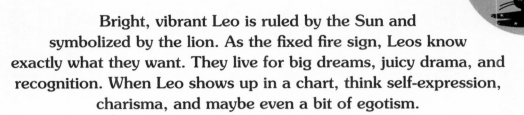

July 23–August 22

Bright, vibrant Leo is ruled by the Sun and symbolized by the lion. As the fixed fire sign, Leos know exactly what they want. They live for big dreams, juicy drama, and recognition. When Leo shows up in a chart, think self-expression, charisma, and maybe even a bit of egotism.

Strengths	Weaknesses	Element	Modality
Courageous, Confident, Generous, Entertaining	Proud, Self-Centered, Obstinate, Vain	Fire	Fixed

Leos are incredibly generous and kindhearted.
Describe a time you shared your abundance with others.

....

....

....

....

....

....

....

VIRGO

August 23–September 22

Ruled by Mercury, Virgo is represented by the
maiden or goddess. Virgo is the mutable earth sign, giving
Virgos the unique ability to strip away the unnecessary and
refine things to perfection. With Virgo placements, think diligence,
practicality, and perhaps even harsh judgments.

Strengths	Weaknesses	Element	Modality
Observant, Selfless, Dedicated, Diligent	Critical, Overthinking, Perfectionist, Micromanaging	Earth	Mutable

**Virgos find peace in setting things right.
What habits or routines center you?**

....

....

....

....

....

....

....

LIBRA

September 23–October 22

Symbolized by the scales of justice and ruled
by Venus, Libras love all things balanced and beautiful.
They are the cardinal air sign, with a desire to create harmony
in all areas of life. When Libra shows up in a chart, think
fairness, charm, and maybe even some indecisiveness.

Strengths	Weaknesses	Element	Modality
Diplomatic, Objective, Amiable, Inclusive	Evasive, Indecisive, People-Pleasing, Resentful	Air	Cardinal

Libras are always taking care of others.
Do you take time to meet your own needs? How?

....

....

....

....

....

....

....

SCORPIO

October 23–November 21

Scorpio is represented by the scorpion and ruled
by both Pluto and Mars. (Pluto in modern astrology, Mars in
classical astrology.) This fixed water sign is inquisitive and magnetic, with
a strong desire for true intimacy, through thick and thin. Where Scorpio
placements are found, think intensity, transformation, and maybe even obsession.

Strengths	Weaknesses	Element	Modality
Devoted, Fearless, Loyal, Accepting	Fixated, Suspicious, Self-Destructive, Nihilistic	Water	Fixed

**Scorpios seek to make deep soul connections.
Who do you feel most connected to? Why do you think that is?**

SAGITTARIUS

November 22–December 21

Ruled by expansive Jupiter, Sagittarius is symbolized
by the archer or centaur archer. This is a mutable fire sign,
constantly on the move like an arrow shot from a bow. Sagittarius is
a lifelong learner, always seeking truth. When Sagittarius shows up in a chart,
think optimism, enthusiasm, and a sometimes-dangerous unpredictability.

Strengths	Weaknesses	Element	Modality
Authentic, Keen, Cheerful, Bold	Unreliable, Unrealistic, Commitment-Wary, Erratic	Fire	Mutable

Sagittariuses love to learn, to expand their horizons.
If you could learn a new skill, what would it be?

....

....

....

....

....

....

....

....

CAPRICORN

December 22–January 19

Capricorn is ruled by Saturn, the planet of discipline.
Like the mythical sea-goat that is their symbol, these cardinal
earth signs are tenacious, able to climb vast mountains of ambition and
delve deeply into the seas of human experience. Where Capricorn placements are
found, think commitment, pragmatism, and perhaps even some impenetrable walls.

Strengths	Weaknesses	Element	Modality
Persevering, Strong Leader, Resourceful, Disciplined	Isolated, Worried, Materialistic, Demanding	Earth	Cardinal

Capricorns thrive on dreaming big and following through on their dreams.
What holds you back from chasing your dreams?

....

....

....

....

....

....

....

....

AQUARIUS

January 20–February 18

The resident revolutionary of the zodiac,
Aquarius is ruled by both Uranus and Saturn. Symbolized
by the water-bearer, Aquarius is known for embracing visionary ideas
and unconventional attitudes. When Aquarius shows up in a chart, think
intellect, community, and sometimes even emotional detachment.

Strengths	Weaknesses	Element	Modality
Clever, Tolerant, Inventive, Curious	Contrarian, Aloof, Rebellious, Indifferent	Air	Fixed

Aquariuses push the boundaries to find the new.
Describe a time you left your comfort zone. What did you learn?

....

....

....

....

....

....

....

PISCES

February 19–March 20

Symbolized by two swimming fish, Pisces is
ruled by both Neptune and Jupiter. This mutable water sign
has a reputation for being dreamy and highly empathetic. Pisces tend to
go with the flow, feeling out situations subjectively. With Pisces placements,
think receptiveness, nurturing, and maybe even a sense of martyrdom.

Strengths	Weaknesses	Element	Modality
Compassionate, Imaginative, Adaptable, Healing	Avoidant, Aimless, Distractable, Lacking Follow-Through	Water	Mutable

**Pisces reach out to connect to everyone and everything.
Does empathy come naturally to you?**

....

....

....

....

....

....

....

....

ELEMENTS

Each astrology sign has an elemental type. There are four kinds of elements in astrology: fire, earth, air, and water. Fire signs burn bright, with a focus on self-expression and enthusiasm. Earth signs are the stabilizers of the zodiac, preferring practical, grounded things. Air signs are all about communication and intellect. Water signs process the world via emotion and intuition.

FIRE: RADIANT ENERGY

Aries, Leo, Sagittarius

Keywords: Spontaneity, Expressiveness, Courage, Forcefulness

What fire placements stand out in your chart?

....

....

....

....

When was the last time you just said YES! to doing something new?

....

....

....

....

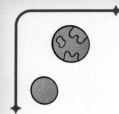

EARTH: GROUNDED ENERGY

Taurus, Virgo, Capricorn

Keywords: Practicality, Sensibility, Dedication, Materialism

What earth placements stand out in your chart?

....

....

....

....

....

....

How do you connect with nature, or wish you could?

....

....

....

....

....

....

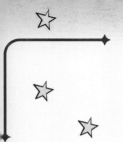

AIR: FRESH ENERGY

Gemini, Libra, Aquarius

Keywords: Communication, Intellect, Charm, Nonchalance

What air placements stand out in your chart?

....

....

....

....

....

Are you more of a talker or a thinker?

....

....

....

....

....

WATER: EMOTIONAL ENERGY

Cancer, Scorpio, Pisces

Keywords: Intuition, Emotions, Sentimentality, Sensitivity

What water placements stand out in your chart?

....

....

....

....

....

Has anyone ever suddenly poured their heart out to you?
Have you done it yourself?

....

....

....

....

....

....

MODALITIES

There are three types of modalities in astrology: cardinal, fixed, and mutable. Think about modality in terms of the seasons. Cardinal signs fall at the beginning of the season and are driven to *do*, to use the energy at their disposal. Fixed signs are right in the middle of the season and are dependable, solid, and centered. Mutable signs are at the end of the season and exist in shifting times as seasons change; they are the best at adapting to change and moving forward. Four seasons, with three signs per season, gives all twelve signs their time to shine!

CARDINAL SIGNS: THE INITIATORS

Aries, Cancer, Libra, Capricorn

Keywords: Energy, Connections, Drive, Beginnings

Where do these signs fall in your chart?

....

....

....

....

Where do you find yourself taking initiative in your life?

....

....

....

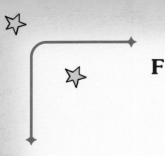

FIXED SIGNS: THE RESOLUTE ONES

Taurus, Leo, Scorpio, Aquarius

Keywords: Constancy, Persistence, Stability, Development

Where do these signs fall in your chart?

....

....

....

....

....

....

In what areas of life do you see yourself as most stubborn or determined?

....

....

....

....

....

....

MUTABLE SIGNS: THE ADAPTERS

Gemini, Virgo, Sagittarius, Pisces

Keywords: Change, Movement, Cooperation, Communication

Where do these signs fall in your chart?

....

....

....

....

....

Your plans have changed at the last minute. How does that make you feel?

....

....

....

....

....

Astrological Check-in

Do you have a strong elemental influence in your chart? Or is it pretty well-balanced? Which modality do you find yourself most drawn to?

No one is just their Sun sign stereotype. What element or modality really spoke to you? Does it differ from your Sun types?

....

....

....

....

....

....

....

....

....

....

COLOR IN YOUR ASTROLOGY CONFIDENCE METER!

| not so confident | mildly confident | super confident |

DIVING DEEPER

Now that you have the basic information about the astrology signs under your belt, let's get into just what they're up to in your birth chart, and, therefore, your life. In this chapter, we will get deeper into astrology and cover the planets and houses of the zodiac.

Since some planets are closer to the Sun than others, they make their way across our skies here on Earth more quickly than those outer planets do. These are your Sun, Moon, and Rising signs, as well as your Mercury, Venus, and Mars signs. In a birth chart, these placements can change very quickly, especially the Rising, or Ascendant, sign. The travel time of the various planets is why your birth time is essential for an accurate natal chart. The rest of the planets are "generational." Jupiter, Saturn, Uranus, Neptune, and Pluto all take much longer to traverse our skies. Jupiter shifts signs once every year or so, while Pluto, with its weird orbit, can linger in a placement for decades! These outer planets affect whole generations and are less personalized.

We all have a planet "in" a sign, which can also be referred to as a placement. Look at your chart. On a standard circular birth chart, you'll see the signs on the outer rim; there are twelve circling the entire wheel. At the moment of your birth, each planet was in a specific place in one of those sections. That's where each placement comes from.

In addition to the twelve parts on the outer rim of your chart known as planets, you also have another twelve divisions in the inner section, where the planets are located. These divisions are known as astrological houses. Each of these houses rules a different area of life. Learning what each house deals with and how your own personal placements fit into each one can give you some serious insight into your life.

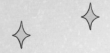

THE PLANETS

For this section, refer back to your birth chart on page 9 and fill in each of your placements. Each planet in our solar system, including the two luminaries (aka the Sun and the Moon), has a role in your life and your personality. What sign is playing the role of the Sun for you? Which one is giving your Moon its own unique flavor? Use this cheat sheet as a quick reference when you're wondering exactly how a certain placement affects your life.

THE SUN

The "planet" of the self, influencing your core personality and ego.

Willpower ★ Expression ★ Pride

My Sun sign:

THE MOON

The "planet" of emotions, influencing your inner self and soul.

Emotions ★ Instincts ★ Memories

My Moon sign:

MERCURY

The planet of communication, influencing your speech and way of thinking.

Communication ★ Intellect ★ Mentality

My Mercury sign:

VENUS

The planet of love and money, influencing what you find romantic and pleasurable.

Romance ★ Beauty ★ Money

> My Venus sign:

MARS

The planet of passion, influencing your drives and how you take action.

Passion ★ Drive ★ Energy

> My Mars sign:

JUPITER

The planet of luck, influencing your fortune and ideologies.

Abundance ★ Luck ★ Knowledge

> My Jupiter sign:

SATURN

The planet of karma, influencing your generation's ideas of discipline and responsibility.

Discipline ★ Challenges ★ Patience

> My Saturn sign:

URANUS

The planet of rebellion, influencing your ideas of freedom and innovation.

Changes ★ Eccentricities ★ Disruptions

My Uranus sign:

NEPTUNE

The planet of illusion and escape, influencing your cultural values.

Dreams ★ Imagination ★ Delusion

My Neptune sign:

PLUTO

The planet of power and transformation, influencing your generation's lasting changes.

Power ★ Death ★ Evolution

My Pluto sign:

HONORARY MENTION: RISING

(also known as your Ascendant sign)

Not a planet, but still a super-important placement, influencing your initial vibe—how others see you. This is the zodiac sign that was on the eastern horizon of the Sun sign during the time you were born.

Persona ★ Actions ★ Appearance

My Rising (Ascendant) sign:

ASTROLOGICAL HOUSES

Knowing your birth time, aka the moment you took your very first breath in our Universe, is absolutely essential for determining house locations. The houses start with your Rising or Ascendant sign, right at the cusp of the First House (page 40), and proceed counterclockwise around your chart from there. Without that key starting point, there's no way to know if your houses, and therefore the placements within those houses, are accurate. Try to get ahold of your birth certificate or ask someone who would know, to make sure to have as accurate a birth time as possible.

We know, we know. It's getting a little more complicated. But we also know that you can totally handle it! Like any practice, astrology takes time to absorb all the juicy details! You just have to keep working with your birth chart. The more comfortable you get looking at it and deciphering all the intricacies of your placements, the more of those "OMG I totally see that," moments you'll have.

Some houses might have multiple placements, while others might have nothing at all. Neither is good or bad, so don't freak out about it! Just take time to reflect on how the excess or lack of placements might affect that area of life. We all have different priorities and ways of moving through life, and that's totally okay.

Cosmic Tip

We use the Placidus method for calculating astrological houses. There are more than thirty different house systems out there, but while it looks a bit complicated, the Placidus method actually has a more astronomically correct view of space and has always felt more accurate to us. In technical terms, the Placidus House System measures the Sun's path across our sky, using different points on the ecliptic to determine where each house begins. Be sure to select the Placidus House System in any birth chart app or calculator you're using.

FIRST HOUSE

Ah, the very first house in your chart! This is by far the easiest one to find, and everyone has a placement in this lovely home: the Ascendant. Look for the left-most point on your birth chart. This point defines the locations of all the other houses, and it's why you need an accurate birth time. This is your front-facing self, the first thing other people see about you. It's the first impression you make on others and your self-image.

YOU

★ Ego ★ Presentation ★ Instincts ★ Temperament ★ Personality ★

Placements in the First House:

....

Choose five words to describe yourself or ask a friend to send you five words that they think describe you and write them down here.

....

....

....

....

....

....

....

SECOND HOUSE

You're nestled into that chart now. The Second House comes next, ruling over material things and your attitudes towards them. This house deals with income, debt, values, and your urge to acquire things.

MONEY & POSSESSIONS

★ Finances ★ Self-Worth ★ Spending and Earning ★ Belongings ★ Values ★

Placements in the Second House:

....

If you were super rich, how would you indulge?
Would you be an extravagant spender or more of a smart investor?

....

....

....

....

....

....

....

....

THIRD HOUSE

Next is the Third House, which rules communication. We're talking (get it?) language, everyday socializing, trips, siblings, and people you interact with on a daily basis.

COMMUNICATION

★ **Connections** ★ **Transportation** ★ **Correspondence** ★ **Language** ★ **Learning** ★

Placements in the Third House:

....

Who is the person in your life that you can talk to about anything? Why?

....

....

....

....

....

....

....

....

....

FOURTH HOUSE

Welcome to the Fourth House, which rules your home and roots. This one is a biggie for tapping into your inner child and your early life experiences. This house also typically influences your relationship with the parent who had the strongest presence in your youth.

The cusp of this house is another of those fancy birth-chart angles: the Imum Coeli, or lower heaven. This is the opposite of the Midheaven (Medium Coeli) point (see page 49). The line that these two points make is your journey from your private roots here in the Fourth House all the way up through to your public calling and accomplishments in the Tenth House.

HOME

★ Ancestors ★ Foundations ★ Parents ★ Traditions ★ Childhood ★

Placements in the Fourth House:

....

Describe your relationship with your parents. How has it shaped you?

....

....

....

....

....

....

....

FIFTH HOUSE

Ah, the Fifth House, aka the house of pleasure! Here, you'll find insight into how you have fun, what you find entertaining, and your hobbies (and obsessions)! Think about your attitude toward games, going out, and casual sex. It's all about play here.

PLEASURE

★ Hobbies ★ Entertainment ★ Fun ★ Romance ★ Casual Sex ★

Placements in the Fifth House:

....

You're on a date. What would have to happen for you to ditch? Or describe your perfect, fun-filled day.

....

....

....

....

....

....

....

....

SIXTH HOUSE

A bit more serious than the last house, the Sixth House rules over your routines and health. It touches on everything from daily hygiene, your sense of duty, and service to others, including pets! Planets found here can influence any work you *have* to do, including necessary everyday self-care.

HEALTH

★ **Healing** ★ **Routines** ★ **Pets** ★ **Self-Care** ★ **Tidiness** ★

Placements in the Sixth House:

....

Describe all the ways you practice self-care. Include both the "fun" ways you do this and the "necessary" ones.

....

....

....

....

....

....

....

....

SEVENTH HOUSE

The Seventh House rules partnerships and relationships. This includes personal relationships, marriages, business partners, bosses, and even enemies! It also deals with legal contracts and formal agreements.

The cusp of the Seventh House is home to another of your birth chart angles: the Descendant or DC. Sitting opposite your Ascendant, this is the sign on the opposite horizon when you were born. It defines the things you seek in your relationships with others, the kinds of people you're drawn to. Think of the Ascendant as "me" and the Descendant as "we."

RELATIONSHIPS

★ **Partnerships** ★ **Contracts** ★ **Social Dynamics** ★ **Enemies** ★ **Connections** ★

Placements in the Seventh House:

....

What role do you usually play in a group?

....

....

....

....

....

....

EIGHTH HOUSE

Taking a turn for the heavy, the Eighth House rules over death, losses, taxes, and the metaphysical. This house also speaks to intimate sex, personal growth, and shared resources and inheritances. It touches on a lot of material points while asking us to acknowledge impermanence and the things you will leave behind.

LOSS & INTIMACY

★ Death ★ Shared Money ★ Sex ★ Transformation ★ The Occult ★

Placements in the Eighth House:

....

Now is the time. Write down what you need to let go.

....

....

....

....

....

....

....

....

NINTH HOUSE

The Ninth House is all about spirituality and expansion. It rules foreign travel and higher learning, both of which expand one's horizons and open the mind to new ways of thinking. The planets found here will impact how you view the world.

SPIRITUALITY

★ **Higher Learning** ★ **Law and Religion** ★ **Foreign Travel** ★ **Expansion** ★ **Beliefs** ★

Placements in the Ninth House:

....

Describe the thing or things for which you have a burning, unquenchable thirst for knowledge.

....

....

....

....

....

....

....

....

TENTH HOUSE

Presiding over the public arena of your life, the Tenth House rules career, ambition, and your reputation. Think callings rather than "just a job," your place in society, and the spheres of influence and power for which you strive.

The cusp of the Tenth House is where you'll find your Midheaven (MC). This point is opposite your *Imum Coeli* (IC), which was found back in the Fourth House. Your Midheaven points to your ideal calling in life, as well as what you define as success.

CAREER & CALLING

★ **Reputation** ★ **Accomplishments** ★ **Public Recognition** ★ **Influence** ★ **Vocation** ★

Placements in the Tenth House:

....

What does your idea of success look like?

....

....

....

....

....

....

....

....

ELEVENTH HOUSE

The Eleventh House rules all things companion-related, such as friendships, communities you're a part of, and social gatherings. Here you'll find insight into your own attitudes surrounding social structures, interactions with other people, and the network that supports you in your hopes and dreams. Charity and altruism fall under the Eleventh House as well.

FRIENDSHIP

★ **Communities** ★ **Altruism** ★ **Friends** ★ **Expectations** ★ **Collaboration** ★

Placements in the Eleventh House:

....

If you're a reflection of the five people you spend the most time with, what does that look like?

....

....

....

....

....

....

....

....

TWELFTH HOUSE

The last, and maybe the most mysterious, is the Twelfth House, ruling over dreams, secrets, addictions, and the subconscious. This is usually a very abstract house, pushing past your social self of the Eleventh House and tapping into your more secret, wild soul.

SECRETS

★ **Hidden Things** ★ **Dreams** ★ **Fantasies** ★ **Subconscious** ★ **Psyche** ★

Placements in the Twelfth House:

....

Describe a fantasy you've never revealed to anyone.

....

....

....

....

....

....

....

....

STELLIUMS

Take a quick look back over your placements. Are you seeing some signs show up in multiple places? Maybe you have multiple planets in a single house? If you have three or more placements residing in the same place, that's called a stellium.

Stelliums are neither good nor bad, but they do mean that you have a stronger influence from that particular sign or in that area of life. Some people find that they don't relate to their Sun sign yet have a ton of energy from a stellium they didn't even realize they had.

Are the recurring planets showing you a major theme in your life?

....

....

....

....

....

....

....

....

....

Where do you see the energy of your signs show up in your life?

YOUR CHART RULER

One more super-important thing to mention: your chart ruler. Look for the planet in charge of your Rising sign. This is the planet or luminary doing the most from behind the scenes. Your astrological makeup is going to be heavily flavored by this celestial body, so pay attention to the vibes of that planet. You might also feel a stronger influence from transits that feature this planet!

Aries Rising	Mars
Taurus Rising	Venus
Gemini Rising	Mercury
Cancer Rising	Moon
Leo Rising	Sun
Virgo Rising	Mercury
Libra Rising	Venus
Scorpio Rising	Mars/Pluto
Sagittarius Rising	Jupiter
Capricorn Rising	Saturn
Aquarius Rising	Saturn/Uranus
Pisces Rising	Jupiter/Neptune

Cosmic Tip

Seeing two "rulers" in your chart? Check both! You're likely to find greater value in the traditional rulers, aka the personal planets. They're more, well, personalized. Pluto, Uranus, and Neptune are generational planets.

What planet is your chart ruler?
And how do you see this showing up in your life?

....

....

....

....

....

....

Which aspect of your chart ruler do you like best?
Which do you like the least?

....

....

....

....

....

....

Astrological Check-in

Did you feel drawn to any planet placement in particular?
What about an astrological house?

....

....

....

....

....

....

....

....

....

....

....

Which house had the most placements for you?
How do you see that manifesting in your life?

....

....

....

....

....

....

....

....

....

....

COLOR IN YOUR ASTROLOGY CONFIDENCE METER!

| not so confident | mildly confident | super confident |

THE ASTROLOGY OF YOU

Give yourself a round of applause, cosmic hottie! You're officially equipped with the tools you need to really start digging into the astrology of you, so let's get into just how the signs influence your life. Each and every sign is part of your life in some form, and the best way to understand how this applies to you is to take a look at the overall vibe of individual signs. This is your journal, so don't be afraid to tap into the more hidden parts, the ones you keep buried under your outer personality. Self-discovery, baby! It's not always comfortable, but growth is always worth it.

Don't be shy about flipping back to chapters one and two whenever you need a bit of a refresher on the traits of certain signs or planets. Make a conscious effort to read your birth chart, too. Find the symbols for each planet, see what sign and house they reside in. The more familiar you get with deciphering a birth chart, the more complete a picture of yourself you'll be able to see.

This is your journey: Take the time to really sit with each component of your chart. Reflect. Let it ruminate. There's literally no rush! Use as much space as you need, both on these pages and in your life. You're a truly unique, transcendent piece of the Universe, after all. And that's absolutely beautiful.

YOUR BIG THREE

When you're just starting out on your astrological journey, it's best to focus on exploring the Big Three placements in your chart. Knowing your Big Three is the best way to kind of ease into the astrology experience. These are the placements that have the greatest influence on your own day-to-day life because they inform so much of how you act and react. They fall under the umbrella of "personal planets," as opposed to "generational planets."

Your Big Three are your Sun sign, Moon sign, and Rising (or Ascendant) sign. They work together to build a *way* more detailed picture than just a Sun sign alone. After all, there are only twelve Sun signs, but Sun/Moon/Rising combinations? That's 1,728 different possibilities, without adding in any other placements! (Tell that to someone next time they say astrology is too simple!) Whether you're delving deep within or just laughing at astrology memes, your Sun, Moon, and Rising signs are important keys to understanding you.

Your Sun sign is the central self, your core identity. Just as that bright, beautiful Sun is the central point of our solar system, your Sun is the anchoring point around which all your other placements revolve. Everything in your chart wraps around that bright, glowing Sun sign! When you check your Sun in an astrology setting, you're looking at the ways you express your individuality, what makes you feel confident, and your self-image. This is an outward-facing placement, something that others see. The Sun has sway over your actions.

Your Moon sign, on the other hand, is your inner self, your emotional identity. The more self-awareness you practice, the more you'll feel connected to your Moon sign. This is a more private, intimate side of your personality. Other people tend to see this only when they are very close to you. Your Moon placement influences your reactions. How you process your feelings and relate to people on an instinctual level is due in large part to your Moon sign. Here, you tend to find insight into the kinds of structures, people, and patterns that allow you to feel a sense of stability in life. This is also a big one for relationship compatibility. When you're trying to figure out how to make someone feel seen and appreciated, check their Moon sign.

The final ingredient in your Big Three is your Rising sign. This placement is also sometimes called the Ascendant because this sign was literally ascending over the eastern horizon when you took your first breath. Your Rising sign is the mask you wear out in the world. These are the traits others see in you, so this sign has a big influence on things like physical appearance, mannerisms, and first impressions. When you see someone and think, oh, they *must* be a Pisces, only to find out they're a Libra Sun or another Sun sign, you might be picking up on their Rising sign.

Not to freak you out or anything, but this is the one that needs you to be as exact as possible with your birth time! Rising signs change every two hours or so, which is why precision is so important. Minutes can make the difference sometimes. The more exact your birth time, the more accurately your Rising sign will reflect you!

YOUR BIG THREE

How do you feel about your Big Three placements?
What feels right to you, and what feels off?

Most people aren't a "typical" version of their Sun sign. In what ways do you feel your Moon and Rising signs influence and transform your Sun sign?

Do you think your placements are accurate to your personality?
Why or why not?

Who are you, darling? Check your Big Three and find out.
Enter in the characteristic that falls under your signs below.

I am

....
(enter Sun sign characteristic)   (enter Moon sign characteristic)

who needs

....
(enter Rising sign characteristic)

	SUN	MOON	RISING
ARIES	a feisty	daredevil	a friendly competition
TAURUS	a vibey	connoisseur	a change of pace
GEMINI	a daring	cheerleader	a pause button
CANCER	a soulful	mermaid	daily self-care
LEO	a radiant	performer	a studio audience
VIRGO	a giving	mastermind	some me time
LIBRA	a delightful	trendsetter	to go with their gut
SCORPIO	an enigmatic	detective	to let people in
SAGITTARIUS	a dynamic	wanderer	to finish what they start
CAPRICORN	a devoted	mogul	to take a break
AQUARIUS	an inspiring	rebel	to be more vulnerable
PISCES	a chill	artist	a long hug

ARIES VIBES

CARDINAL FIRE SIGN

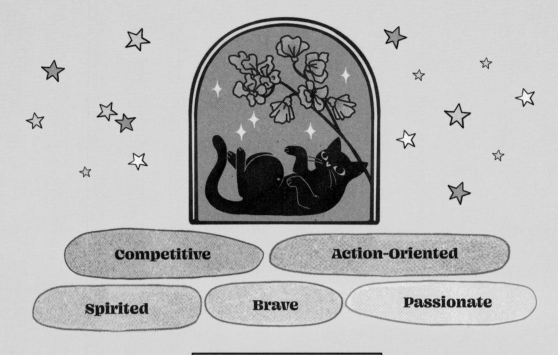

Competitive

Action-Oriented

Spirited

Brave

Passionate

RULED BY MARS

Where do you have Aries in your chart?
Does this fiery sign appear in any planets or houses?

What is something you've always wanted to start doing?

....

....

....

....

....

....

In what areas of life could you use some more Aries courage?

....

....

....

....

....

....

TAURUS VIBES

FIXED EARTH SIGN

Charming

Down-to-Earth

Persistent

Sensual

Blissful

RULED BY VENUS

Where do you have Taurus in your chart?
Does this earthy sign appear in any planets or houses?

Everybody needs a safe place to chill out in. What would be your absolute utopia if money, travel, or atmospheric limits didn't apply?

....

....

....

....

....

....

....

In what areas of life could you use some more Taurus tenacity?

....

....

....

....

....

....

....

GEMINI VIBES

MUTABLE AIR SIGN

Energetic Expressive

Funny Versatile Keen

RULED BY MERCURY

Where do you have Gemini in your chart?
Does this airy sign appear in any planets or houses?

Think about your social circle. What kinds of social situations give you energy? Which drain you? Do you identify more as an introvert or an extrovert?

....

....

....

....

....

....

In what areas of life could you use some more Gemini flexibility?

....

....

....

....

....

....

CANCER VIBES

CARDINAL WATER SIGN

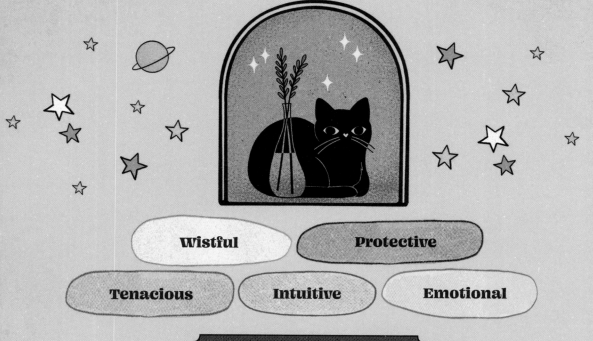

Wistful

Protective

Tenacious

Intuitive

Emotional

RULED BY THE MOON

Where do you have Cancer in your chart?
Does this watery sign appear in any planets or houses?

**Describe an emotional experience that ultimately
created a better relationship for you.**

....

....

....

....

....

....

....

In what areas of life could you use some more Cancer compassion?

....

....

....

....

....

....

LEO VIBES

FIXED FIRE SIGN

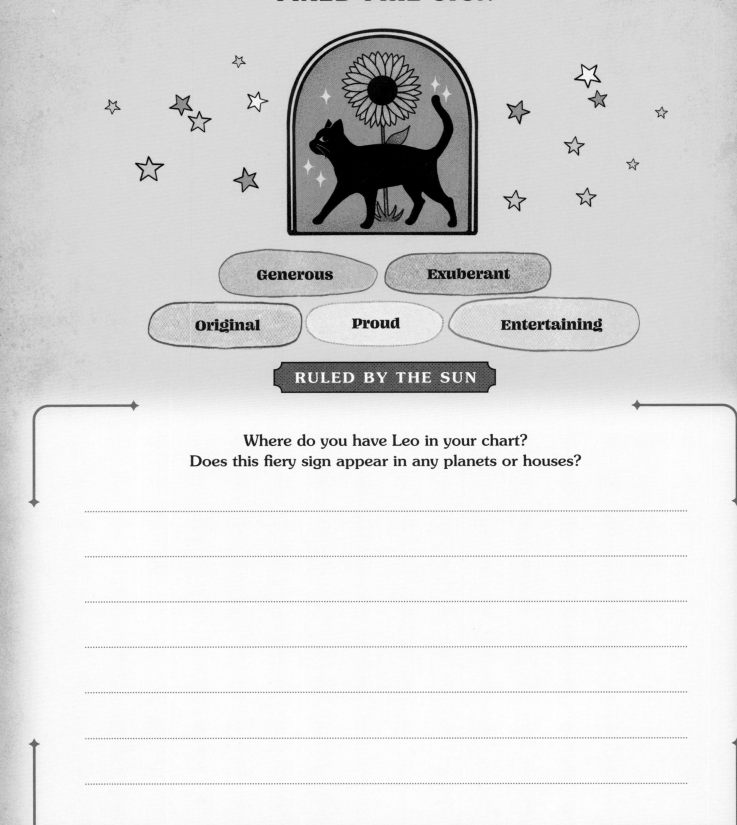

Generous

Exuberant

Original

Proud

Entertaining

RULED BY THE SUN

Where do you have Leo in your chart?
Does this fiery sign appear in any planets or houses?

When was the last time you had to summon all your courage? How did it turn out?

....

....

....

....

....

....

In what areas of life could you use some more Leo fearlessness?

....

....

....

....

....

VIRGO VIBES

MUTABLE EARTH SIGN

Bright   **Dedicated**

Precise   **Observant**   **Giving**

RULED BY MERCURY

Where do you have Virgo in your chart?
Does this earthy sign appear in any planets or houses?

....

....

....

....

....

....

How can you cleanse your life? What can you let go of to make things better?

....

....

....

....

....

....

....

In what areas of life could you use some more Virgo dedication?

....

....

....

....

....

....

LIBRA VIBES

CARDINAL AIR SIGN

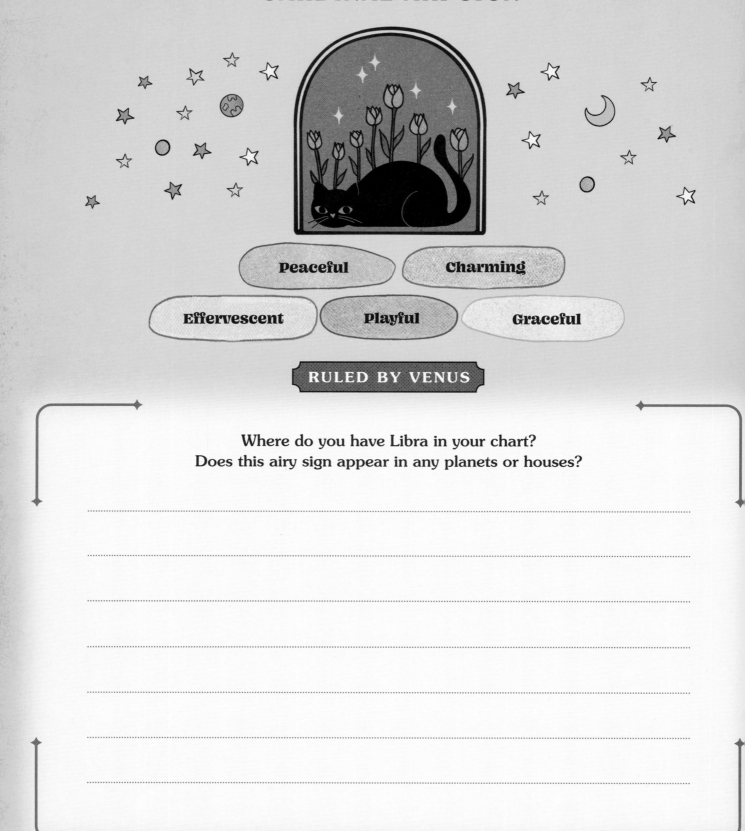

Peaceful

Charming

Effervescent

Playful

Graceful

RULED BY VENUS

Where do you have Libra in your chart?
Does this airy sign appear in any planets or houses?

....

....

....

....

....

....

How do you show up for others? Where do you fall short in showing up for *you*?

In what areas of life could you use some more Libra diplomacy?

SCORPIO VIBES

FIXED WATER SIGN

Transformative

Dedicated

Mysterious

Beguiling

Fearless

RULED BY MARS AND PLUTO

Where do you have Scorpio in your chart?
Does this watery sign appear in any planets or houses?

What's a non-negotiable for you? What will you never change your mind about?

....

....

....

....

....

....

In what areas of your life could you use more Scorpio curiosity?

....

....

....

....

....

....

SAGITTARIUS VIBES

MUTABLE FIRE SIGN

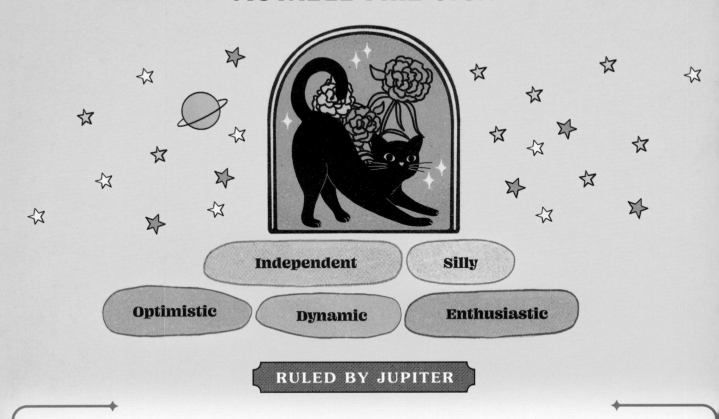

Independent **Silly**

Optimistic **Dynamic** **Enthusiastic**

RULED BY JUPITER

Where do you have Sagittarius in your chart?
Does this fiery sign appear in any planets or houses?

Let's talk commitment: do you jump right in with your whole heart?
Or are you more wary of long-term plans?

In what areas of life could you use some more Sagittarius adventure?

CAPRICORN VIBES

CARDINAL EARTH SIGN

Resourceful   **Witty**

Brilliant   **Classy**   **Determined**

RULED BY SATURN

Where do you have Capricorn in your chart?
Does this earthy sign appear in any planets or houses?

....

....

....

....

....

....

....

Are you a self-starter? What's the best project you've ever poured your heart into?

....

....

....

....

....

....

....

In what areas of life could you use some more Capricorn follow-through?

....

....

....

....

....

....

....

AQUARIUS VIBES

FIXED AIR SIGN

Individualistic

Quirky

Visionary

Curious

Genuine

RULED BY URANUS AND SATURN

Where do you have Aquarius in your chart?
Does this airy sign appear in any planets or houses?

What's a cause you really believe in? How can you get more involved in it?

....

....

....

....

....

....

In what areas of life could you use some more Aquarius innovation?

....

....

....

....

....

PISCES VIBES

MUTABLE WATER SIGN

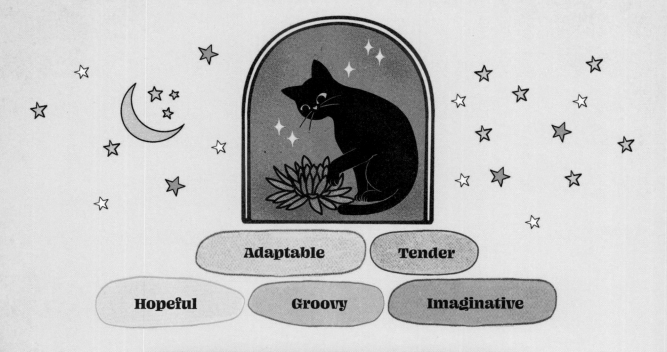

Adaptable

Tender

Hopeful

Groovy

Imaginative

RULED BY NEPTUNE AND JUPITER

Where do you have Pisces in your chart?
Does this watery sign appear in any planets or houses?

....

....

....

....

....

....

Do you have any strange, secret hobbies? Does anyone know about them?

....

....

....

....

....

....

....

In what areas of life could you use some more Pisces empathy?

....

....

....

....

....

....

....

Astrological Check-in

How's it going? Are you getting more comfortable with the star signs?

How can you use what you've learned about astrology thus far to make constructive changes in your life?

....

....

....

....

....

....

....

....

....

....

COLOR IN YOUR ASTROLOGY CONFIDENCE METER!

| not so confident | mildly confident | super confident |

COMPATIBILITY

When something is tons of fun (and eerily accurate!), we know we like to share it with other people. Raise your hand if you're guilty of hitting up everyone for their birth date and time the more you get into astrology.

We get it. It's exciting to see how you and your besties mesh together cosmically! And since we're looking to get to know ourselves better through astrology, it's pretty essential that we learn about how we interact with different placements.

When we're talking compatibility, it's super important to keep in mind how complex just *one* birth chart is. Add in another birth chart or two and you'll be getting closer to the reality of human interaction: complicated, involved, sometimes thorny, and sometimes amazing. Compatibility is way, way more than just two Sun signs vibing well. There's an entire branch of astrology dedicated to synastry—where an astrologer will overlay two birth charts and study the placements and aspects within that relationship. Yeah, it gets super elaborate, but you don't need to do that to have some fun figuring out how you relate to different people, thankfully!

Get all those essential, juicy astro details on the folks you love: birth date, time, and place. Generate their birth charts and save 'em or screenshot 'em. It's time to dip your toe in some compatibility fun!

YOUR RELATIONSHIP STYLE

Look to your Venus sign when love and intimacy are on the table. This lush, loving sign is all about the things you value, as well as your aesthetic preferences.

Your Venus Sign: ....

How do you react when you start to fall for someone?

TURN-ONS AND TURN-OFFS

Everything in your chart is always working together. Here, we're looking at the combo of your Venus and Mars. What makes you swoon? What makes you cringe? What's the elemental and modality balance like? If you're all earth-based here, it's likely you're going to totally hate unrealistic, unpredictable behavior.

VENUS SIGN

....

....
Modality   Element

MARS SIGN

....

....
Modality   Element

Make a list of the little gestures and traits that other people do that make your heart skip a beat.

....

....

....

....

....

....

....

....

Make a list of some behavior or mannerisms that other people do that absolutely horrify you.

It's date night! What would make it totally perfect?
Take us through the day from start to finish.

BEST FRIENDS, FAMILY, LOVERS ... ANYONE!

Write down the names, birthdays, and signs of your loved ones in the table below.

Note: Even without a birth time, you should be able to find someone's Sun and Moon signs with their birth date, since the Moon stays in one sign for a few days at a time. It can change, though, in which case you might need to read about the Moon sign particulars and decide which is right for your person.

Person	Birth Date	Sun Sign	Moon Sign	Rising Sign

Who in your group do you mesh with best?
How do their signs harmonize with yours?

....

....

....

....

....

....

Who do you have to put in more effort with? How do your signs vibe?

....

....

....

....

....

ZODIAC SIGN COMPATIBILITY

Whether it's a bestie or a life partner, it's just the *best* feeling to find someone you totally click with. Some signs just vibe with each other better than others because they share similar ways of interacting with the world or value the same things. Compare your signs with your favorite people to puzzle out why you guys just work so dang well!

Legend:
- ♥ OMG soulmates
- ♥ Matching energies
- ♥ Totally in sync
- ♥ Opposites attract
- ♥ Different energies
- ♥ It's a struggle
- ♥ Not for me

	Aries ♈	Taurus ♉	Gemini ♊	Cancer ♋	Leo ♌	Virgo ♍	Libra ♎	Scorpio ♏	Sagittarius ♐	Capricorn ♑	Aquarius ♒	Pisces ♓
Aries ♈	♥	♥	♥	♥	♥	♥	♥	♥	♥	♥	♥	♥
Taurus ♉	♥	♥	♥	♥	♥	♥	♥	♥	♥	♥	♥	♥
Gemini ♊	♥	♥	♥	♥	♥	♥	♥	♥	♥	♥	♥	♥
Cancer ♋	♥	♥	♥	♥	♥	♥	♥	♥	♥	♥	♥	♥
Leo ♌	♥	♥	♥	♥	♥	♥	♥	♥	♥	♥	♥	♥
Virgo ♍	♥	♥	♥	♥	♥	♥	♥	♥	♥	♥	♥	♥
Libra ♎	♥	♥	♥	♥	♥	♥	♥	♥	♥	♥	♥	♥
Scorpio ♏	♥	♥	♥	♥	♥	♥	♥	♥	♥	♥	♥	♥
Sagittarius ♐	♥	♥	♥	♥	♥	♥	♥	♥	♥	♥	♥	♥
Capricorn ♑	♥	♥	♥	♥	♥	♥	♥	♥	♥	♥	♥	♥
Aquarius ♒	♥	♥	♥	♥	♥	♥	♥	♥	♥	♥	♥	♥
Pisces ♓	♥	♥	♥	♥	♥	♥	♥	♥	♥	♥	♥	♥

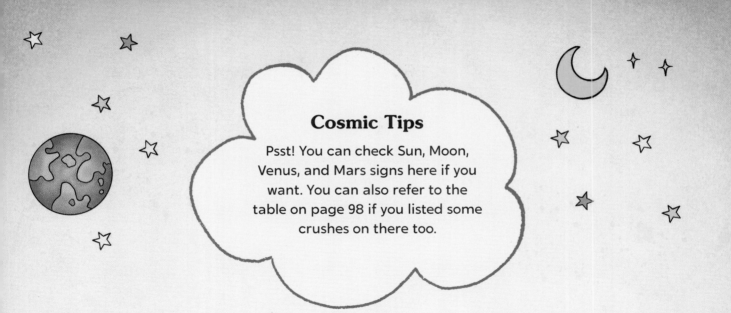

Cosmic Tips

Psst! You can check Sun, Moon, Venus, and Mars signs here if you want. You can also refer to the table on page 98 if you listed some crushes on there too.

Person's Name	Sun Sign Compatibility	Moon Sign Compatibility	Rising Sign Compatibility	Venus Sign Compatibility	Mars Sign Compatibility	Overall Compatibility (circle one)
	♡	♡	♡	♡	♡	Yes No It's complicated
	♡	♡	♡	♡	♡	Yes No It's complicated
	♡	♡	♡	♡	♡	Yes No It's complicated
	♡	♡	♡	♡	♡	Yes No It's complicated
	♡	♡	♡	♡	♡	Yes No It's complicated

Astrological Check-in

What matchup were you most surprised by?

Are there any signs you're now more willing to give the benefit of the doubt?

....

....

....

....

....

....

....

....

....

COLOR IN YOUR ASTROLOGY CONFIDENCE METER!

| not so confident | mildly confident | super confident |

ASTROLOGY FUN

Astrology—right?! The more you learn, the more you're kind of blown away by it. As a full-fledged cosmic hottie, you totally get it by now: Astrology is complex, nuanced, and fascinating. There's literally *so much* to the practice of astrology. Getting familiar with your placements can give you incredible insight into your own psyche, revealing the things you need to feel safe and loved, the kinds of traits you're drawn to, how to approach both the big and the little things in life . . . and that's just scratching the surface.

With that said, we'd like to take a quick minute to point out another super-useful part of astrology: the good old-fashioned fun of it! Yes, it's true: you can get really academic with astrology and still use it to just straight up have a good time.

For this section, let your mind wander. Take time to simply sit and be present, doing whatever you happen to be doing. Of course, delving into your soul and your motivations is extremely beneficial, but it's not *exactly* the most relaxing activity! Don't stress yourself out breaking down the minutia of what's in this section. Just . . . enjoy.

PLANETARY PLAYLIST

Craft a playlist that totally encapsulates your zodiac signs!

_____

_____

_____

_____

_____

_____

_____

_____

_____

_____

_____

_____

_____

Cosmic Tip

Feel free to make your playlist on Spotify, or wherever, and share it with us! Just tag us on social: @thepulpgirls.

COMMUNICATION, BABY!

Hey, we're humans. We *need* communication and mental stimulation. That doesn't mean we all think and speak in the exact same ways, though. One person might need time and space to consider their words, while another cuts right to the heart of a matter. Where's your mind at, honey?

Your Mercury Sign:

....

Cosmic Tip

Mercury signs are never more than one sign away from your Sun. So, it can only be either a match to your Sun sign, or the sign before or after it. Use this cool fact to guess people's Mercury sign if you know their Sun.

Do you feel like you have to rush and get your words out ASAP?
Or are you more measured and thoughtful with your words?

....

....

....

....

....

....

IT'S A MATCH!

Flex that astrology knowledge, cosmic hottie!
Match the signs with the vibe that you think fits them.

Cosmic Tip

Don't forget, you can always flip back to the zodiac sign section on pages 12 to 24.

The Idea Maker

Positive traits: Likeable, visionary, and paradoxical

Negative traits: Hates fads, lack of freedom, and clinginess

The Action Star

Positive traits: Bold, dynamic, and fearless

Negative traits: Hates delays, timid people, and restrictions

Taurus

Aries

Libra

The Starry-Eyed Spirit

Positive traits: Peace-loving, reserved, and imaginative

Negative traits: Hates crowds, tension, and insensitivity

Leo

Cancer

Gemini

The Enigmatic Enchantress

Positive traits: Mystifying, resolute, and unforgettable

Negative traits: Hates half-truths, prying eyes, and uninformed opinions

The Elf Princess

Positive traits: Whimsical, otherworldly, and contemplative

Negative traits: Hates reality, stressful situations, and making a decision

The Fearless Magician

Positive traits: Positive, enthusiastic, and proud

Negative traits: Hates complainers, disrespect, and sitting it out

The Young at Heart

Positive traits: Unpredictable, witty, and full of life

Negative traits: Hates monotony, sensitivity, and choosing one thing

The Chill Wanderer

Positive traits: Restless, optimistic, and tolerant

Negative traits: Hates bummers, feeling confined, and tedium

Aquarius

Virgo

Capricorn

The Truth-Teller

Positive traits: Sincere, caring, and a bit aloof

Negative traits: Hates avoidable mistakes, ignorance, and recklessness

Pisces

Sagittarius

Scorpio

The Tranquil Artist

Positive traits: Peaceful, luxurious, and trustworthy

Negative traits: Hates unreliability, chaos, and being corrected

The Charming Fairy

Positive traits: Gracious, stylish, and magnetic

Negative traits: Hates violence, gauche things, and being alone

The Old Soul

Positive traits: Pensive, indomitable, and honest

Negative traits: Hates fickleness, clueless people, and unfinished tasks

♓	Pisces: The Elf Princess
♒	Aquarius: The Idea Maker
♑	Capricorn: The Old Soul
♐	Sagittarius: The Chill Wanderer
♏	Scorpio: The Enigmatic Enchantress
♎	Libra: The Charming Fairy
♍	Virgo: The Truth-Teller
♌	Leo: The Fearless Magician
♋	Cancer: The Starry-Eyed Spirit
♊	Gemini: The Young at Heart
♉	Taurus: The Tranquil Artist
♈	Aries: The Action Star

Answer Key:

ASTROLOGICAL SOUL SEARCHING

WAIT! Before you start seeking out all the words possible in this word search, close your eyes. Take a few deep breaths, in and out . . . turn your mind perfectly smooth and rounded, like a ball. Allow all your thoughts to slip away from the surface of your mind, and just . . . relax. Now, with your mind and body calm and centered, look at the word search. What word or words immediately call out to you?

I	A	S	T	S	E	H	R	S	S	I	I
N	Y	O	E	N	T	O	E	A	T	E	N
L	I	R	N	O	E	N	S	F	A	V	T
V	N	I	A	A	D	E	O	E	B	I	U
R	T	G	C	T	R	S	L	T	I	S	I
I	E	I	I	U	A	T	V	Y	L	I	T
T	N	N	T	A	M	Y	E	U	I	O	I
V	S	A	Y	G	A	E	E	T	T	N	O
W	I	L	L	P	O	W	E	R	Y	I	N
T	T	I	P	L	E	A	S	U	R	E	O
F	Y	T	T	U	H	P	E	A	C	E	R
U	S	Y	N	J	O	Y	J	N	R	S	T
N	L	L	V	S	P	I	O	T	S	E	T
L	A	W	A	R	E	N	E	S	S	T	I

What three words did you see first?

1. ....

2. ....

3. ....

Do these words call to mind any particular placements right now?
What is your subconscious asking you to pay attention to?

....

....

....

....

....

....

....

....

....

Answer Key: Stability, Willpower, Intuition, Hope, Tenacity, Joy, Resolve, Pleasure, Peace, Awareness, Intensity, Drama, Safety, Originality, Honesty, Fun, Vision

TAROT CARDS FOR THE SIGNS

Did you know that each astrology sign has a Major Arcana tarot card that totally vibes with it? Yep! Each tarot card has specific archetypes depicted in it that align with the archetypes of the zodiac. We've got twelve of our very own Pulp Tarot cards here for you, along with a bit of insight into just how they fit each sign.

ARIES

THE EMPEROR

A powerful figure, positively brimming
with authority and bad-babe vibes.

Ruled by Mars	Ram Throne	Crown
Potency and Determination	Power and Self-Assurance	Leadership and Influence

Where in life does it feel natural for you to take charge?

....

....

....

List three things that make you feel empowered.

1. ....

2. ....

3. ....

TAURUS

THE HIEROPHANT

A dedicated figure, unafraid of hard work,
poised to achieve truly great things.

Ruled by Venus	Keys	Raised Hand
Love and Beauty	Path to Higher Self	Guidance and Strength

What practices cultivate your inner strength?

....

....

....

....

....

....

....

List three traditions that you draw on in life.

1. ....

2. ....

3. ....

GEMINI

THE LOVERS

Two figures, representing variety, considering things
from all angles, and diverse energies.

Ruled by Mercury	Angel	Duality
Energy and Spirit	Blessings and Protection	Other Perspectives

What are you truly committed to?

....

....

....

....

....

....

List three things you're grateful for right now.

1. ....

2. ....

3. ....

CANCER

THE CHARIOT

A warrior figure rushing toward victory,
overcoming any and all obstacles in their path.

Ruled by the Moon	Armor	Sphinxes
Hope and Inspiration	Protection and Courage	Finding Oneself

How has your ego evolved over time?

....

....

....

....

....

....

List three places where you want to go.

1. ....

2. ....

3. ....

LEO

STRENGTH

A compassionate figure extending a helping hand,
exuding staying power and confidence.

Ruled by the Sun	Infinity	Lion
Energy and Spirit	Limitless Possibility	Passion and Perseverance

Do you trust in your abilities?

....

....

....

....

....

....

List three things you love about yourself.

1. ....

2. ....

3. ....

VIRGO

THE HERMIT

A pensive figure taking time to reflect, seeking a deeper understanding of life, and looking inward.

Ruled by Mercury	Lantern	The Number 9
Thought and Discovery	Clarity and Understanding	Spiritual Awakening

What is your relationship with solitude?

....

....

....

....

....

....

List three things you prefer to do alone.

1. ....

2. ....

3. ....

LIBRA

JUSTICE

A balanced figure, taking every opinion,
weighing the scales, and delivering a compromise.

Ruled by Venus	Scales	Sword
Charm and Peace	Truth and Balance	Impartiality and Intelligence

What causes would you go to bat for?

....

....

....

....

....

....

....

List three parts of your life that need more balance.

1. ....

2. ....

3. ....

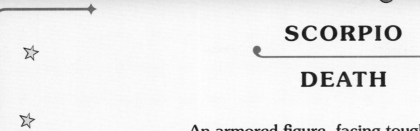

SCORPIO

DEATH

An armored figure, facing tough changes,
ushering in new beginnings and transformation.

Ruled by Pluto	Flag	Rising Sun
Change and Upheaval	Beauty and Purification	Possibilities Ahead

What endings in your life have given birth to new beginnings?

....

....

....

....

....

....

List three ways you renew your energy.

1. ....

2. ....

3. ....

SAGITTARIUS

TEMPERANCE

A peaceful figure, with one foot on the ground and
the other dipping into the waters of the spiritual realm.

Ruled by Jupiter	Chalice	Path
Joy and Clarity	Intuition and Flow of Life	Adventure of Life

What is your relationship to creativity?

....

....

....

....

....

....

....

List three extremes you want to address.

1. ....

2. ....

3. ....

CAPRICORN

THE DEVIL

A winged figure perched above two people, representing power and the drive necessary to achieve ambitions.

Ruled by Saturn	Wings	Pedestal
Power and Authority	Free Will and Drive	Independence and Elevation

Do you allow yourself to indulge?

....

....

....

....

....

....

....

List three of your guilty pleasures.

1. ....

2. ....

3. ....

AQUARIUS

THE STAR

A serene figure, lit by the brightest star in the sky, pouring forth creativity and assurance.

Ruled by Uranus	Morningstar	Waters
Innovation and Discovery	Hope and Direction	Flowing Imagination

What does self-love mean to you?

....

....

....

....

....

....

List three things that always make you smile.

1. ....

2. ....

3. ....

PISCES

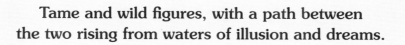

THE MOON

Tame and wild figures, with a path between
the two rising from waters of illusion and dreams.

Ruled by Neptune	Moon	Crustacean
Instinct and Mystery	Cycles and Reflection	Subconscious and Dreams

Do you find meaning in your dreams?

....

....

....

....

....

....

....

List three recurring symbols from your dreams.

1. ....

2. ....

3. ....

Astrological Check-in

How are you feeling about your understanding of astrology now?

....

....

....

....

....

....

....

....

....

....

....

How can you use your understanding of your own astrological makeup
to make positive changes moving further?

....

....

....

....

....

....

....

....

....

....

COLOR IN YOUR ASTROLOGY CONFIDENCE METER!

| not so confident | mildly confident | super confident |

ASTROLOGICAL OCCURRENCES

Everything in this wide, beautiful Universe happens in cycles—from the tiniest things to the cosmic forces swirling around us. The wheel is always turning, seasons come and go, the signs cycle through the astrological year, and planets orbit around the Sun. It won't surprise you to hear that a lot of astrology involves paying attention to recurring events.

With all the planets exerting an influence on our lives, there are a lot of transits (planetary movements) at play on any given day. All of those movements then interact with your individual natal chart, which can mean anything from experiencing weird moods to sudden bursts of creativity, or even just adding a bit of a different vibe to your day.

The planets with the most transits are those closest to us here on Earth: The Sun, the Moon, Mercury, Mars, and Venus. (Psst! That's also why they're referred to as the personal planets!) The outer planets, or generational planets, tend to have longer-lasting effects because they happen more rarely.

With an entire solar system of potential transits out there, it's best to focus on the most common ones when you're an astro newbie. This entire section is devoted to New Moons, Full Moons, and the dreaded Mercury Retrogrades. These astrological occurrences can vary year to year, but typically there are twelve New Moons, twelve Full Moons, and three Mercury Retrogrades a year. Use these pages to get a feel for the energies of each astrological occurrence. You can learn a lot about yourself by doing a self-vibe check during each of these cyclical events throughout the year. Track your goals, see how you've grown, and find your center! You got this, babe.

NEW MOON VIBE CHECK

New Moons, or Dark Moons, are all about fresh starts. During these lunations, focus on **intentions**. This is the time to add a new routine or set new goals for the coming cycle. What do you want to bring into being in the next few weeks, months, or even years?

Each New Moon occurs in one of the zodiac signs. Use an app or the internet to look up the sign this New Moon is in and write it down here:

....

INTENTIONS	ACTION PLAN
What dreams or goals are you manifesting?	Magic requires intention and action! Write out three actionable steps you can take toward your goals.

1. ....

....

....

2. ....

....

....

3. ....

....

....

1. ....

....

....

2. ....

....

....

3. ....

....

....

FULL MOON VIBE CHECK

Full Moons are all about completion. During these lunations, focus on **reflection**. This is the time to check in on goals that you set in the past, to examine what works for you and what doesn't. What can you release in order to make space for the new?

Each Full Moon occurs in one of the zodiac signs. Use an app or the internet to look up the sign this Full Moon is in and write it down here:

....

INTENTIONS

What goals are you closer to achieving?

ACTION PLAN

List three ways you've progressed on your goals.

1.
....

....

....

2.
....

....

....

3.
....

....

....

1.
....

....

....

2.
....

....

....

3.
....

....

....

NEW MOON VIBE CHECK
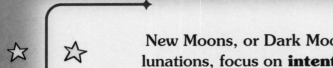

New Moons, or Dark Moons, are all about fresh starts. During these lunations, focus on **intentions**. This is the time to add a new routine or set new goals for the coming cycle. What do you want to bring into being in the next few weeks, months, or even years?

Each New Moon occurs in one of the zodiac signs. Use an app or the internet to look up the sign this New Moon is in and write it down here:

....

INTENTIONS	**ACTION PLAN**
What dreams or goals are you manifesting?	Magic requires intention and action! Write out three actionable steps you can take toward your goals.

1. ....

....

....

2. ....

....

....

3. ....

....

....

1. ....

....

....

2. ....

....

....

3. ....

....

....

FULL MOON VIBE CHECK

Full Moons are all about completion. During these lunations, focus on **reflection**. This is the time to check in on goals that you set in the past, to examine what works for you and what doesn't. What can you release in order to make space for the new?

Each Full Moon occurs in one of the zodiac signs. Use an app or the internet to look up the sign this Full Moon is in and write it down here:

....

INTENTIONS

What goals are you closer to achieving?

1.

....

....

....

2.

....

....

....

3.

....

....

ACTION PLAN

List three ways you've progressed on your goals.

1.

....

....

....

2.

....

....

....

3.

....

....

NEW MOON VIBE CHECK

New Moons, or Dark Moons, are all about fresh starts. During these lunations, focus on **intentions**. This is the time to add a new routine or set new goals for the coming cycle. What do you want to bring into being in the next few weeks, months, or even years?

Each New Moon occurs in one of the zodiac signs. Use an app or the internet to look up the sign this New Moon is in and write it down here:

....

INTENTIONS

What dreams or goals are you manifesting?

ACTION PLAN

Magic requires intention and action! Write out three actionable steps you can take toward your goals.

1. ....

....

....

2. ....

....

....

3. ....

....

1. ....

....

....

2. ....

....

....

3. ....

....

FULL MOON VIBE CHECK

Full Moons are all about completion. During these lunations, focus on **reflection**. This is the time to check in on goals that you set in the past, to examine what works for you and what doesn't. What can you release in order to make space for the new?

Each Full Moon occurs in one of the zodiac signs. Use an app or the internet to look up the sign this Full Moon is in and write it down here:

....

INTENTIONS

What goals are you closer to achieving?

ACTION PLAN

List three ways you've progressed on your goals.

1.
....

....

....

2.
....

....

....

3.
....

....

1.
....

....

....

2.
....

....

....

3.
....

....

NEW MOON VIBE CHECK

New Moons, or Dark Moons, are all about fresh starts. During these lunations, focus on **intentions**. This is the time to add a new routine or set new goals for the coming cycle. What do you want to bring into being in the next few weeks, months, or even years?

Each New Moon occurs in one of the zodiac signs. Use an app or the internet to look up the sign this New Moon is in and write it down here:

....

INTENTIONS

What dreams or goals are you manifesting?

ACTION PLAN

Magic requires intention and action! Write out three actionable steps you can take toward your goals.

1. ....

....

....

2. ....

....

....

3. ....

....

....

1. ....

....

....

2. ....

....

....

3. ....

....

....

FULL MOON VIBE CHECK

Full Moons are all about completion. During these lunations, focus on **reflection**. This is the time to check in on goals that you set in the past, to examine what works for you and what doesn't. What can you release in order to make space for the new?

Each Full Moon occurs in one of the zodiac signs. Use an app or the internet to look up the sign this Full Moon is in and write it down here:

....

INTENTIONS

What goals are you closer to achieving?

ACTION PLAN

List three ways you've progressed on your goals.

1.
....

....

....

2.
....

....

....

3.
....

....

....

1.
....

....

....

2.
....

....

....

3.
....

....

....

NEW MOON VIBE CHECK

New Moons, or Dark Moons, are all about fresh starts. During these lunations, focus on **intentions**. This is the time to add a new routine or set new goals for the coming cycle. What do you want to bring into being in the next few weeks, months, or even years?

Each New Moon occurs in one of the zodiac signs. Use an app or the internet to look up the sign this New Moon is in and write it down here:

....

INTENTIONS

What dreams or goals are you manifesting?

ACTION PLAN

Magic requires intention and action! Write out three actionable steps you can take toward your goals.

1. ....

....

....

2. ....

....

....

3. ....

....

1. ....

....

....

2. ....

....

....

3. ....

....

FULL MOON VIBE CHECK

Full Moons are all about completion. During these lunations, focus on **reflection**. This is the time to check in on goals that you set in the past, to examine what works for you and what doesn't. What can you release in order to make space for the new?

Each Full Moon occurs in one of the zodiac signs. Use an app or the internet to look up the sign this Full Moon is in and write it down here:

....

INTENTIONS
What goals are you closer to achieving?

ACTION PLAN
List three ways you've progressed on your goals.

1. ....

....

....

2. ....

....

....

3. ....

....

....

1. ....

....

....

2. ....

....

....

3. ....

....

....

NEW MOON VIBE CHECK

New Moons, or Dark Moons, are all about fresh starts. During these lunations, focus on **intentions**. This is the time to add a new routine or set new goals for the coming cycle. What do you want to bring into being in the next few weeks, months, or even years?

Each New Moon occurs in one of the zodiac signs. Use an app or the internet to look up the sign this New Moon is in and write it down here:

....

INTENTIONS

What dreams or goals are you manifesting?

1. ....

....

....

2. ....

....

....

3. ....

....

....

ACTION PLAN

Magic requires intention and action! Write out three actionable steps you can take toward your goals.

1. ....

....

....

2. ....

....

....

3. ....

....

....

FULL MOON VIBE CHECK

Full Moons are all about completion. During these lunations, focus on **reflection**. This is the time to check in on goals that you set in the past, to examine what works for you and what doesn't. What can you release in order to make space for the new?

Each Full Moon occurs in one of the zodiac signs. Use an app or the internet to look up the sign this Full Moon is in and write it down here:

....

INTENTIONS	ACTION PLAN
What goals are you closer to achieving?	List three ways you've progressed on your goals.

1.
....

....

2.
....

....

3.
....

....

NEW MOON VIBE CHECK

New Moons, or Dark Moons, are all about fresh starts. During these lunations, focus on **intentions**. This is the time to add a new routine or set new goals for the coming cycle. What do you want to bring into being in the next few weeks, months, or even years?

Each New Moon occurs in one of the zodiac signs. Use an app or the internet to look up the sign this New Moon is in and write it down here:

....

INTENTIONS

What dreams or goals are you manifesting?

ACTION PLAN

Magic requires intention and action! Write out three actionable steps you can take toward your goals.

1. ....
....
....

1. ....
....
....

2. ....
....
....

2. ....
....
....

3. ....
....
....

3. ....
....
....

FULL MOON VIBE CHECK

Full Moons are all about completion. During these lunations, focus on **reflection**. This is the time to check in on goals that you set in the past, to examine what works for you and what doesn't. What can you release in order to make space for the new?

Each Full Moon occurs in one of the zodiac signs. Use an app or the internet to look up the sign this Full Moon is in and write it down here:

....

INTENTIONS

What goals are you closer to achieving?

ACTION PLAN

List three ways you've progressed on your goals.

1. ....

....

....

2. ....

....

....

3. ....

....

1. ....

....

....

2. ....

....

....

3. ....

....

NEW MOON VIBE CHECK

New Moons, or Dark Moons, are all about fresh starts. During these lunations, focus on **intentions**. This is the time to add a new routine or set new goals for the coming cycle. What do you want to bring into being in the next few weeks, months, or even years?

Each New Moon occurs in one of the zodiac signs. Use an app or the internet to look up the sign this New Moon is in and write it down here:

....

INTENTIONS	**ACTION PLAN**
What dreams or goals are you manifesting?	Magic requires intention and action! Write out three actionable steps you can take toward your goals.

1. ....   1. ....

....

....

2. ....   2. ....

....

....

3. ....   3. ....

....

....

FULL MOON VIBE CHECK

Full Moons are all about completion. During these lunations, focus on **reflection**. This is the time to check in on goals that you set in the past, to examine what works for you and what doesn't. What can you release in order to make space for the new?

Each Full Moon occurs in one of the zodiac signs. Use an app or the internet to look up the sign this Full Moon is in and write it down here:

....

INTENTIONS

What goals are you closer to achieving?

ACTION PLAN

List three ways you've progressed on your goals.

1.
....

....

....

2.
....

....

....

3.
....

....

1.
....

....

....

2.
....

....

....

3.
....

....

NEW MOON VIBE CHECK

New Moons, or Dark Moons, are all about fresh starts. During these lunations, focus on **intentions**. This is the time to add a new routine or set new goals for the coming cycle. What do you want to bring into being in the next few weeks, months, or even years?

Each New Moon occurs in one of the zodiac signs. Use an app or the internet to look up the sign this New Moon is in and write it down here:

....

INTENTIONS

What dreams or goals are you manifesting?

1. _____

....

....

2. _____

....

....

3. _____

....

....

ACTION PLAN

Magic requires intention and action! Write out three actionable steps you can take toward your goals.

1. _____

....

....

2. _____

....

....

3. _____

....

....

FULL MOON VIBE CHECK

Full Moons are all about completion. During these lunations, focus on **reflection**. This is the time to check in on goals that you set in the past, to examine what works for you and what doesn't. What can you release in order to make space for the new?

Each Full Moon occurs in one of the zodiac signs. Use an app or the internet to look up the sign this Full Moon is in and write it down here:

....

INTENTIONS

What goals are you closer
to achieving?

ACTION PLAN

List three ways you've
progressed on your goals.

1. ....

....

....

2. ....

....

....

3. ....

....

....

1. ....

....

....

2. ....

....

....

3. ....

....

....

NEW MOON VIBE CHECK

New Moons, or Dark Moons, are all about fresh starts. During these lunations, focus on **intentions**. This is the time to add a new routine or set new goals for the coming cycle. What do you want to bring into being in the next few weeks, months, or even years?

Each New Moon occurs in one of the zodiac signs. Use an app or the internet to look up the sign this New Moon is in and write it down here:

....

INTENTIONS

What dreams or goals are you manifesting?

ACTION PLAN

Magic requires intention and action! Write out three actionable steps you can take toward your goals.

1. ....

....

....

2. ....

....

....

3. ....

....

1. ....

....

....

2. ....

....

....

3. ....

....

FULL MOON VIBE CHECK

Full Moons are all about completion. During these lunations, focus on **reflection**. This is the time to check in on goals that you set in the past, to examine what works for you and what doesn't. What can you release in order to make space for the new?

Each Full Moon occurs in one of the zodiac signs. Use an app or the internet to look up the sign this Full Moon is in and write it down here:

....

INTENTIONS

What goals are you closer
to achieving?

1.
....

....

....

2.
....

....

....

3.
....

....

....

ACTION PLAN

List three ways you've
progressed on your goals.

1.
....

....

....

2.
....

....

....

3.
....

....

....

NEW MOON VIBE CHECK

New Moons, or Dark Moons, are all about fresh starts. During these lunations, focus on **intentions**. This is the time to add a new routine or set new goals for the coming cycle. What do you want to bring into being in the next few weeks, months, or even years?

Each New Moon occurs in one of the zodiac signs. Use an app or the internet to look up the sign this New Moon is in and write it down here:

....

INTENTIONS

What dreams or goals are you manifesting?

1. ....

....

....

2. ....

....

....

3. ....

....

ACTION PLAN

Magic requires intention and action! Write out three actionable steps you can take toward your goals.

1. ....

....

....

2. ....

....

....

3. ....

....

FULL MOON VIBE CHECK

Full Moons are all about completion. During these lunations, focus on **reflection**. This is the time to check in on goals that you set in the past, to examine what works for you and what doesn't. What can you release in order to make space for the new?

Each Full Moon occurs in one of the zodiac signs. Use an app or the internet to look up the sign this Full Moon is in and write it down here:

....

INTENTIONS	ACTION PLAN
What goals are you closer to achieving?	List three ways you've progressed on your goals.

1. ....

....

....

2. ....

....

....

3. ....

....

....

1. ....

....

....

2. ....

....

....

3. ....

....

....

NEW MOON VIBE CHECK

New Moons, or Dark Moons, are all about fresh starts. During these lunations, focus on **intentions**. This is the time to add a new routine or set new goals for the coming cycle. What do you want to bring into being in the next few weeks, months, or even years?

Each New Moon occurs in one of the zodiac signs. Use an app or the internet to look up the sign this New Moon is in and write it down here:

....

INTENTIONS	**ACTION PLAN**
What dreams or goals are you manifesting?	Magic requires intention and action! Write out three actionable steps you can take toward your goals.

1.
....

....

2.
....

....

3.
....

....

FULL MOON VIBE CHECK

Full Moons are all about completion. During these lunations, focus on **reflection**. This is the time to check in on goals that you set in the past, to examine what works for you and what doesn't. What can you release in order to make space for the new?

Each Full Moon occurs in one of the zodiac signs. Use an app or the internet to look up the sign this Full Moon is in and write it down here:

....

INTENTIONS	**ACTION PLAN**
What goals are you closer to achieving?	List three ways you've progressed on your goals.

1. ....

....

....

2. ....

....

....

3. ....

....

....

1. ....

....

....

2. ....

....

....

3. ....

....

....

MERCURY RETROGRADE SURVIVAL GUIDE

Approximately three times a year, Mercury goes retrograde. In planetary terms, it means that Mercury appears to slide backwards across our sky. It doesn't actually reverse its orbit; it's a trick of the eye thanks to the orbits of Earth and Mercury. Astrologically, however, Mercury Retrograde brings in its wake all kinds of confusion, discord, and general mayhem. Sounds kinda scary, right? Don't stress, it's actually a very good time to take a step back and reflect.

Cosmic Tips

Make sure to look up the dates—they're different for each retrograde. Also, what does "stations" even mean, you may ask? It's a fancy astrological way of saying "goes," or "moves."

Mercury Stations Retrograde: ....

Mercury Stations Direct: ....

**What situations, projects, or relationships need to be revisited?
What inner work needs to be addressed?**

....

....

....

....

....

....

....

....

....

....

....

Mercury Stations Retrograde: ....

Mercury Stations Direct: ....

What situations, projects, or relationships need to be revisited?
What inner work needs to be addressed?

....

....

....

....

....

....

....

....

....

....

....

....

....

Mercury Stations Retrograde: ....

Mercury Stations Direct: ....

What situations, projects, or relationships need to be revisited?
What inner work needs to be addressed?

....

....

....

....

....

....

....

....

....

....

....

....

Astrological Check-in

Do you see a pattern or notice any shifts in your mood when the New Moon or Full Moon is on a particular sign, or when it's in any of your Big Three signs?

How do you prepare for Mercury Retrograde?

....

....

....

....

....

....

....

....

....

....

COLOR IN YOUR ASTROLOGY CONFIDENCE METER!

| not so confident | mildly confident | super confident |

WHAT'S NEXT?

Okay. First things first: Thank you so, so much for coming on this incredible ride with us. We truly love and appreciate you so much for diving into the gorgeous, wonderful world of astrology with us. Hopefully you've learned a lot about not only the stars, but also about *you!*

So, what now? Stay the course, honey! There's always more to learn in astrology. Keep up with the planetary transits that happen on the reg. Get a professional astrology reading. Pay attention to your daily horoscope. Incorporate New Moon and Full Moon rituals into your life. As mentioned earlier in the introduction, feel free to use these templates more than once and if you run out of paper, use your personal journal or a separate piece of paper.

Looking for more?
We gotchu, baby! Get the companion book to this workbook, and our tarot deck.

Astrology for the Cosmic Soul
A Modern Guide to the Zodiac

and

The Pulp Girls Tarot Deck
A 78-card Deck of Magic and Affirmations

ABOUT THE AUTHORS

Cailie and Brianna are the co-founders of The Pulp Girls. They are two sisters making magic with vintage art and astrology.

Cailie is The Pulp Girls' resident illustrator. You'll find her gorgeous artwork all over this book. She draws artistic inspiration from all sorts of different outlets: Vintage fashion illustration, advertising, graphics, fairy tales, art zines . . . you name it! Plus, she's a Taurus Sun, Capricorn Moon, and Libra Rising. In case you're new to astrology, those are some strong Venus vibes, meaning she's got quite the aesthetic sense!

Brianna has always had a way with words, pairing expression and creation with a captivating voice. She's an Aries Sun, Pisces Moon, and Leo Rising. She's always found inspiration in fantasy worlds and the occult. Such a Pisces Moon!

Super-important astrological necessity: Follow us on social! We are **@thepulpgirls** on, like, everything. We regularly post astrological info about what's going on in the cosmos, as well as super-cute art for daily life. Plus, we will love you forever and ever!

© 2023 by Quarto Publishing Group USA Inc.
Text and Illustrations © 2023 by The Pulp Girls, Inc.

First published in 2023 by Rock Point, an imprint of The Quarto Group,
142 West 36th Street, 4th Floor, New York, NY 10018, USA
T (212) 779-4972 F (212) 779-6058 www.Quarto.com

Rock Point titles are also available at discount for retail, wholesale, promotional,
and bulk purchase. For details, contact the Special Sales Manager by email
at specialsales@quarto.com or by mail at The Quarto Group, Attn: Special Sales
Manager, 100 Cummings Center Suite 265D, Beverly, MA 01915 USA.

10 9 8 7 6 5 4 3 2 1

ISBN: 978-1-63106-913-0

Publisher: Rage Kindelsperger
Creative Director: Laura Drew
Managing Editor: Cara Donaldson
Editor: Keyla Pizarro-Hernández
Cover and Interior Design: Evelin Kasikov

Printed in China

This workbook provides general information on astrological concepts that tend to
evoke feelings of strength and confidence. However, it should not be relied upon
as recommending or promoting any specific diagnosis or method of treatment for
a particular condition, and it is not intended as a substitute for medical advice or
for direct diagnosis and treatment of a medical condition by a qualified physician.
Readers who have questions about a particular condition, possible treatments for that
condition, or possible reactions from the condition or its treatment should consult a
physician or other qualified healthcare professional.